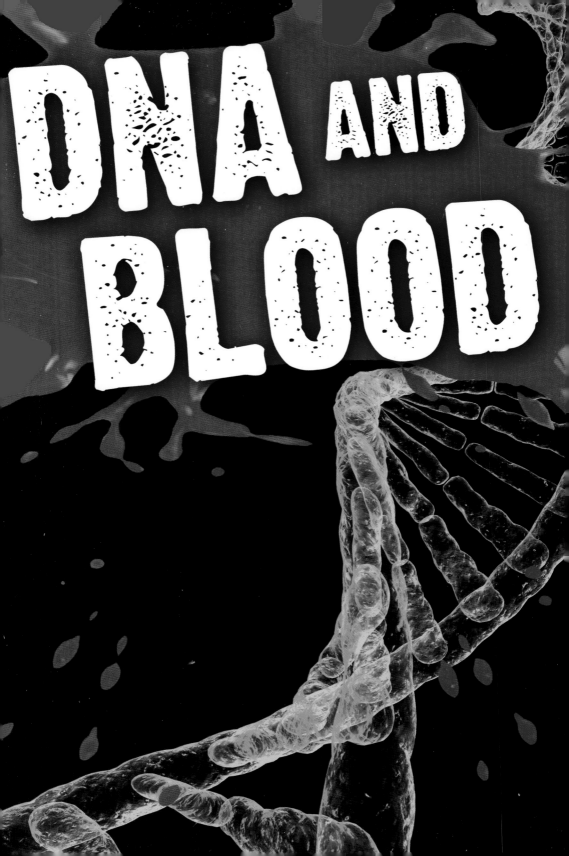

Titles in the True Forensic Crime Stories series:

BONES
DEAD PEOPLE DO TELL TALES
Library Ed. ISBN 978-0-7660-3669-7
Paperback ISBN 978-1-59845-363-8

CYBERCRIME
DATA TRAILS DO TELL TALES
Library Ed. ISBN 978-0-7660-3668-0
Paperback ISBN 978-1-59845-361-4

DNA AND BLOOD
DEAD PEOPLE DO TELL TALES
Library Ed. ISBN 978-0-7660-3667-3
Paperback ISBN 978-1-59845-362-1

FINGERPRINTS
DEAD PEOPLE DO TELL TALES
Library Ed. ISBN 978-0-7660-3689-5
Paperback ISBN 978-1-59845-364-5

GUN CRIMES
DEAD PEOPLE DO TELL TALES
Library Ed. ISBN 978-0-7660-3763-2
Paperback ISBN 978-1-59845-365-2

TRACE EVIDENCE
DEAD PEOPLE DO TELL TALES
Library Ed. ISBN 978-0-7660-3664-2
Paperback ISBN 978-1-59845-366-9

TRUE
forensic
CRIME
stories

DNA AND BLOOD

Dead People DO Tell tales

Sara L. Latta

Enslow Publishers, Inc.
40 Industrial Road
Box 398
Berkeley Heights, NJ 07922
USA
http://www.enslow.com

Library of Congress Cataloging-in-Publication Data

Latta, Sara L.
  DNA and blood : dead people do tell tales / Sara L. Latta.
    p. cm. — (True forensic crime stories)
  Includes bibliographical references and index.
  Summary: "Learn how blood and DNA are used to solve crimes, with real cases as examples"—Provided by
publisher.
  ISBN 978-0-7660-3667-3
  1. Criminal investigation—Case studies—Juvenile literature. 2. Forensic hematology—Case studies
—Juvenile literature. 3. DNA fingerprinting—Case studies—Juvenile literature. 4. Forensic sciences—
Case studies—Juvenile literature. I. Title.
  HV8073.8.L38 2012
  363.25'62—dc22
                        2010039474

Paperback ISBN 978-1-59845-362-1

Printed in China

052011 Leo Paper Group, Heshan City, Guangdong, China

10 9 8 7 6 5 4 3 2 1

Photo Credits: Associated Press, pp. 6, 8, 11, 46, 55, 57, 58, 60, 66–67; © GEOATLAS, p. 82;
iStockphoto.com/Rich Legg, p. 68; Library of Congress, p. 25; © 2011 Photos.com, a Division of
Getty Images. All rights reserved., p. 31; Photo Researchers, Inc.: Biophoto Associates, p. 56, BSIP,
p. 50, © Carlyn Iverson, p. 28, Dr. Jurgen Scriba, p. 92, © Jim Varney, pp. 13, 16, 27, Library of
Congress, p. 75, RIA Novosti, p. 74, Ted Kinsman, p. 35, Tek Image, p. 42; Shutterstock.com, pp. 1,
3, 5, 6 (background), 19, 20, 23, 29, 33, 36, 40–41, 48, 52, 62, 78, 84, 86, 88.

Cover Photo: Shutterstock.com

Contents

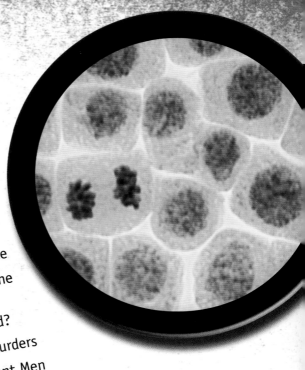

Dr. Sam Sheppard was accused of murdering his wife, Marilyn, in 1954.

Marilyn Sheppard

Blood Evidence

Sam Sheppard and his wife, Marilyn, lived in a well-to-do suburb of Cleveland, Ohio. Sheppard, like his father and brothers, was a doctor. Together they ran Bay View Hospital, which was nearby. Dr. and Mrs. Sheppard had some friends over for dinner on the night of July 3, 1954. It had been a busy day for Dr. Sheppard. He had performed a scheduled surgery in the morning as well as an emergency surgery that afternoon in an unsuccessful attempt to save the life of a young boy who had been hit by a truck. He was called back to the hospital as he and his guests were having predinner cocktails, this time to tend to a boy with a broken leg. Finally, after a late dinner, the guests left around midnight. Dr. Sheppard, exhausted from the day's events, had fallen asleep on the daybed in the living room. Mrs. Sheppard went upstairs to their bedroom.

Just before dawn, Spencer Houk's phone rang. "For God's sake, Spen, get over here!" Houk recognized the voice of his friend and neighbor, Sam Sheppard. "I think they've killed Marilyn."[1] Houk, who also happened to be the mayor of Bay Village, and his wife, Esther, arrived at the Sheppard home a few minutes later. Mrs. Houk found Mrs. Sheppard's bloody body upstairs.

The police were soon on the scene. They questioned Dr. Sheppard briefly, and he told them that he had been awakened by his wife's cries. He headed upstairs to the bedroom, where he had caught a glimpse of a figure wearing a light-colored shirt before being hit on the back of the neck. When he came to, he found his wife lying in a pool of **blood** on the bed, and the bedroom was flecked with red **spatters**. He checked for her pulse. There was none. His seven-year-old son, Chip, slept soundly in his bedroom.

According to Dr. Sheppard, he had heard a noise below. He ran down the stairs just in time to see someone running toward the lake behind his home. He chased the man, whom he would later describe as about six feet three inches tall and middle-aged with bushy hair. He reached the man, and, after a struggle, had been knocked out again. When he awoke, the intruder was gone—this time for good.

Marilyn Sheppard was murdered in her
home while her family was asleep.

Dr. Sheppard claimed to have suffered a neck injury in the scuffle. He clearly had bruises and cuts on his face.

Satisfied, the police allowed Dr. Sheppard's brother to take him to Bay View Hospital to treat his injuries. Chip was sent to the house of another uncle. Soon the house and lawn were crowded with reporters and other curious people; some were even allowed to enter the bedroom where Mrs. Sheppard's body still lay. The crime scene investigators were lax when it came to gathering fingerprints. They photographed the bedroom and some footprints they found outside the house, but on the whole they seemed to regard the crime scene as little more than a bloody mess.

The police and coroner found that Mrs. Sheppard had thirty-five wounds, including fifteen blows to the head, and cuts on her hands, arms, and fingers.

The police were inclined to think that Dr. Sheppard had murdered his wife. It was a reasonable suspicion. At least 30 percent of women who are murdered are killed by people they know—usually a husband or boyfriend.[2] The local newspapers, initially sympathetic to Dr. Sheppard, turned on him. They published editorials, such as one titled "The Finger of Suspicion," that were aimed at the doctor. At the case's **inquest**, it was revealed that Dr. Sheppard had been having an affair with a medical technician at Bay View Hospital. By now most of Cleveland—if not the nation—thought that the wealthy, good-looking doctor was guilty of his wife's murder. Three weeks after the murder, Dr. Sheppard was arrested and charged with the crime.

Dr. Sheppard's trial began on October 18, 1954. His **defense attorney**, William Corrigan, asked for a change of venue. The intense and biased media coverage would make it impossible for his client to get a fair hearing, he said. The judge denied his request.

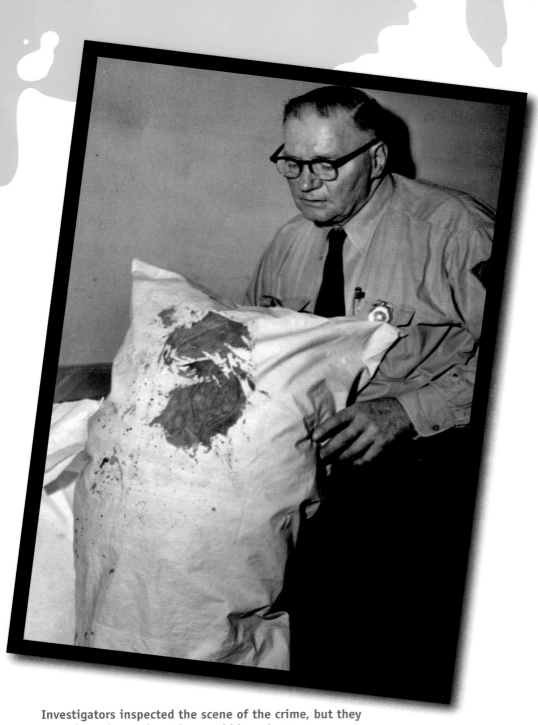

Investigators inspected the scene of the crime, but they weren't as thorough as they could have been.

At the trial, the **prosecuting attorney** said that Dr. Sheppard's story was too far-fetched. How could an intruder have entered the house without waking up the Sheppards? Why hadn't the dog barked? Most incriminating of all was the testimony of the medical technician, Susan Hayes, who said that she and Dr. Sheppard had been having an affair for three years. After six weeks of testimony, the jury found Dr. Sheppard guilty of **second-degree murder**. He was sentenced to life in prison.

Corrigan had made a big mistake in not having his team's own experts examine the house. He tried to correct that mistake after Dr. Sheppard's conviction by calling in a nationally-known expert on what was then a little-known field of forensic science—**bloodstain pattern analysis**. The expert, Paul Kirk, agreed to take on the assignment but warned that he might only find further evidence of Dr. Sheppard's guilt.

Kirk measured and analyzed the shape of hundreds of blood drops in the Sheppards' bedroom. The walls were spattered with blood, except in one corner of the room. Something had blocked the flying drops of blood. That something must have been the killer's own body. He would have been covered with blood spatters. But save for the small bloodstain on his pants, Dr. Sheppard hadn't had any blood on him after the murder. Kirk also noticed an unusual bloodstain on the closet door that was much larger than the other spatters. He could tell from the large size of the stain that it could have traveled only inches before hitting the door. It couldn't have come from the bed where Mrs. Sheppard had been lying. Kirk deduced that Mrs. Sheppard, in a desperate struggle for her life, had wounded the killer.

The police had found two of Mrs. Sheppard's teeth on the bed underneath her body, even though the autopsy had showed that there had been no blow that would have knocked her teeth in. Kirk did some

Forensic scientists use blood spatters to figure out what type of weapon was used in a crime and from how far away.

experiments with teeth he had gotten from dentists. He determined that Mrs. Sheppard's teeth must have been pulled from the inside out. Kirk proposed that Mrs. Sheppard had sunk her teeth into the killer's hand, perhaps as he tried to cover her mouth to stifle her cries. The killer must have ripped her teeth out as he snatched his hand away. Investigators at the time hadn't found any bite marks or other injuries on Dr. Sheppard's hands.

Knowing where the murderer had stood, Kirk could tell from the direction of the blood spatter to the attacker's left that the blows had been delivered from the left side. Unless the killer had used a backhanded stroke—something Kirk thought unlikely, given the angle of the blood spatter—he had delivered the blows with his left hand. Dr. Sheppard was right-handed.

The theory of a wounded killer also explained the blood trail leading out of the bedroom, down the stairs, and out of the house. The prosecution claimed that Dr. Sheppard had carried the weapon through the house, dripping blood as he went. But Kirk showed that it was impossible for a murder weapon to retain enough blood to have created such a long trail—forty drops of blood. The blood must have come from the injured killer, he said.

Kirk also carried out blood-typing tests on the blood spots. He knew that Mrs. Sheppard had type O blood; Dr. Sheppard's was type A. The results were inconclusive, in part because it was difficult to use the technology available at the time to determine blood type in such old samples.

Kirk wrote up his findings in a report with this conclusion: "Taken together, the only explanation that actually is consistent with all the facts is the one given by Sam, vague and uncertain though it may be."[3]

Corrigan submitted the report to the judge. He asked for a new trial based on this new evidence. His request was denied.

Sam Sheppard spent the next ten years in prison, even as Corrigan continued to try to get a new trial. When Corrigan died in 1961, the Sheppard family hired a rising young lawyer named F. Lee Bailey to take on Dr. Sheppard's case. Bailey argued before the U.S. Supreme Court that his client had not been given a fair trial. The court agreed, and in 1966 Dr. Sheppard was granted a second trial.

This time, Kirk was the star witness for the defense. The blood evidence was enough to convince the jury, who returned the **verdict** "Not guilty."

Sam Sheppard was a free man. But the murder trial and publicity had made it impossible for Dr. Sheppard to continue his medical practice. Many people still

WHAT ARE DNA AND BLOOD FORENSICS?

The word *forensic* comes from a Latin word referring to the forum, or a place of public discussion. Public speaking and debate are often called forensics. The term *forensic science* has come to mean science that is discussed in a court of law or in the justice system. At the scene of a crime, there is usually some kind of biological evidence left behind. It may be in the form of blood, saliva, hair, skin cells, sweat, or even teardrops. Forensic scientists may use this evidence and more to figure out what happened at the crime scene, as was the case with the Marilyn Sheppard murder. By analyzing the **proteins** and DNA in blood and other biological evidence, forensic biologists can often learn a lot about the identities of the victim and the criminal.

BLOODSTAIN PATTERN ANALYSIS

To an expert's trained eye, bloodstains can provide valuable clues about how—or whether—a crime was committed. When a drop of blood hits a surface, it leaves a stain with a distinctive shape. Passive bloodstains are created when blood drips to a surface from gravity alone. This is the type of stain a man might leave if he had cut his hand and left a trail of blood drops on the floor as he walked to the sink to wash and bandage his wound. For another example, the stream of blood that flows out of a chest wound would trickle straight down the body if a victim were standing, but veer to the left if he were lying on his left side.

Transfer stains occur when wet blood on one surface comes into contact with another surface. Bloody footprints, fingerprints, or the smear of blood from a body being dragged across the floor are all examples of transfer stains. Projected stains are made when blood is propelled to a surface under a force greater than gravity alone. Blood that spurts from a severed artery is one example. Wounds created by a gunshot, knife, or blunt object—such as a baseball bat—create spatter patterns.

The shapes of these bloodstains can reveal critical information, such as:

- The general direction a drop of blood was traveling at the time of impact, the approximate **angle of impact**, and the approximate distance it traveled
- The potential weapon, and how forcefully it may have been used
- The approximate number of blows struck
- The possible sequence of events during the attack
- The possible position and movements of the victim and attacker
- Whether the attacker may have been left- or right-handed
- The approximate time the attack took place
- Signs indicating whether death was immediate or delayed

Bloodstain pattern analysis experts may spend hours or even days carefully documenting and measuring the size and shape of bloodstains, as well as calculating the distance traveled and angle of impact of each drop of blood. They may attach strings to each individual blood spatter to see where they come together, or converge. They use their knowledge of math to determine the origin of the blood spatters. They may enter all the measurements made at the crime scene into a specialized computer program. One type of program uses all the information to create three-dimensional models and animations that show how and where the bloodstains were made. These can be especially useful for blood pattern analysis experts who are presenting evidence to a jury.

believed he was guilty. He turned to alcohol and drugs, and died of liver failure just four years later.

Chip Sheppard—or Samuel Reese Sheppard, as he preferred to be called as an adult—spent years trying to clear his father's name. Even though his father was found not guilty, that only meant that the jury had reasonable doubt that he had committed the crime. Mr. Sheppard wanted to show that his father was actually innocent. This is a much more difficult thing to prove in a court of law.

In 1999, Mr. Sheppard sued the State of Ohio for the wrongful imprisonment of his father. He had **DNA** tests carried out on old samples of his parents' blood as well as on a sample of blood from a man he believed had committed the crime, Richard Eberling. However, the samples had been collected decades before DNA testing had been developed, long before scientists knew how to preserve blood evidence without contamination. The test results were not conclusive. In 2000, after a ten-week trial, a civil jury declared that Samuel Reese Sheppard had failed to prove that his father had been wrongfully imprisoned.

The Sheppard case marked an important milestone in acknowledging the role of bloodstain evidence in the legal system. It continues to be highly controversial in the Cleveland area. Mrs. Sheppard's killer has never been found.

DNA

DNA, or deoxyribonucleic acid, is a molecule that carries a set of instructions. These instructions tell our cells what to do, which determines physical traits, such as eye color or height. The information encoded on the DNA molecule is what makes a person unique. These instructions are in lengthy stretches of DNA called **genes**. Nearly all the genome is identical for all humans. About 0.1 percent of the **genome** is unique to each individual (except for identical twins, who share the same genome). It is these variable sequences that DNA experts target when analyzing blood, hair, or other biological evidence. They use the data to create a DNA profile, or DNA fingerprint, of an individual. The chances that two unrelated people will share the exact same DNA profile is estimated to be 1 in 1.7 million billion!

The Case of the Bloody Carpenter

On a fall day in 1898, in the quiet little German village of Lechtingen, Hannelore Heidemann and Else Langemeier failed to return from school. The girls' worried mothers visited the school, only to learn that the friends had not been to classes that day. The villagers searched the nearby woods for the girls. Finally, as daylight was fading, someone found Hannelore's murdered body lying among some trees. A short time later, Else's remains were found.

The police learned that a stranger had been seen entering the village from the woods. The man, Ludwig Tessnow, wore an apron that appeared to be stained with some dark liquid. Upon questioning, Tessnow explained that he was a carpenter. The stains were simply a wood dye. To test his claim, a policeman visited Tessnow in his workshop, "accidentally" knocking over a tin of wood dye onto Tessnow's pants. It looked exactly like the stains on the carpenter's apron. The police concluded that he was telling the truth. More experienced crime investigators might have used a microscope to look at the fresh stains on his apron, but it didn't occur to the small town's police force. If they had done so, they would have seen telltale signs of red blood cells.

The villagers persuaded themselves that the girls had been the victims of a hungry wolf. Wolf attacks tended to happen in the winter when food was scarce and the animals were starving. Perhaps it was easier for the villagers to believe this over the alternative.

Tessnow left Lechtingen early the next year. The villagers didn't know where he went; perhaps, remembering the cloud of suspicion surrounding the carpenter, they were simply glad to see him go.

Two and a half years later, strange things began to happen near Göhren, a village on an island off the northern coast of Germany. A farmer found seven of his sheep killed with their bodies mutilated. The farmer had seen a man running away from his farm. He swore he would be able to recognize him if he saw him again. Three weeks later, Hermann Stubbe and his brother, Peter, left their home to play. They never came home.

Their bodies were found shortly after sunrise the following morning. Their skulls had been crushed with a rock.

A villager remembered that he had seen the two boys talking to the odd carpenter Tessnow the day they had disappeared. The police searched Tessnow's home and found clothing and boots with dark

Bloodstains on clothing can be an important
form of evidence.

stains, all recently washed. It was all part of the trade, Tessnow insisted. The stains were simply caused by wood dye.

The village judge recalled the killings in Lechtingen several years earlier and contacted the police there. Yes, they said, the murders had been grisly indeed. Their main suspect was a carpenter named Ludwig Tessnow, but he had sworn that the stains on his clothing had been caused by wood dye. Meanwhile, the farmer whose sheep had been hacked to pieces had no trouble picking Tessnow out of a lineup.

The judge, Johann-Klaus Schmidt, was sure that Tessnow was their man. But how could they prove it? Schmidt's friend, a prosecutor named Ernst Hubschmann, recalled reading a report about a new scientific test for human bloodstains. The test could detect bloodstains even on clothing that had been washed. What's more, it could distinguish between human blood and animal blood.

They sent a package containing some of Tessnow's stained clothes and a bloodstained rock that was believed to be the murder weapon to Paul Uhlenhuth, who was the author of the new scientific article. Uhlenhuth and his assistant painstakingly examined each and every stain on the clothing. They dissolved them in water or salt solutions, testing them for **hemoglobin**, an iron-containing protein in blood that carries oxygen throughout the body. Many of the stains were indeed wood dye. But twenty-six were definitely bloodstains: They contained hemoglobin. By using his new human-protein test, Uhlenhuth was able to show that seventeen of those bloodstains were from human blood. The other seven were from sheep's blood.

Never again would a murderer get away with the claim that the blood of his victims was something other than blood, or that it was the blood of an animal. Ludwig Tessnow was found guilty of the murders. He was put to death three years later.

Is It Human Blood?

In 1885, Louis Pasteur saved the life of a boy who had been bitten by a rabid dog by injecting him with a weakened version of the deadly rabies virus. This was the birth of a new science called immunology. Scientists realized that when a foreign protein (**antigen**) enters the bloodstream, the body makes its own proteins (**antibodies**) that bind to and neutralize it. Emil von Behring found that if he injected egg white into a guinea pig, the animal developed a defensive reaction specific for egg white proteins. What's more, if he added egg white to some of the inoculated animal's **serum** in a test tube, the antibodies bound to the antigens and formed a milky white precipitate.

In 1900, scientist Paul Uhlenhuth from Vienna, Austria, carried out a series of experiments in which he injected chicken blood into rabbits. When he added a drop of chicken blood to a test tube of serum from the inoculated rabbits, the liquid turned cloudy. But when blood from cows, pigs, sheep,

Louis Pasteur

IS IT BLOOD?

If you find someone lying in a pool of red liquid flowing from a hole in his chest, you can be pretty sure that the liquid is blood (unless, of course, that person happens to be an actor on a movie set). But what if you found a crumpled T-shirt with rust-colored stains stashed behind the bushes near a murder scene? Without a good test for blood, it would be difficult to determine whether the wearer is guilty of murder—or simply of the lesser crime of being a sloppy eater. For centuries criminals were literally able to get away with murder because no one could prove that dried bloodstains were, in fact, blood.

As early as 1853, a German scientist found that by adding an acid and a salt to a drop of blood and heating the mixture, crystals would form. This test, as with all tests for blood, depends on the presence of hemoglobin in red blood cells.

Today, forensic scientists have additional reliable presumptive tests for blood. One, called the Kastle-Meyer test, uses a chemical indicator, phenolphthalein, and hydrogen peroxide. The hydrogen peroxide reacts with hemoglobin to create water plus a highly reactive form of oxygen. This form of oxygen reacts with the indicator molecule, changing it from colorless to bright pink.

Modern forensic scientists might also test the stain or scene of a crime with luminol. Luminol is a chemical that gives off a faint bluish glow when it reacts with hemoglobin and hydrogen peroxide. It is so sensitive that it can detect bloodstains on clothing that has been machine-washed. Even if the murderer scrubs down the crime scene, it is nearly impossible to get rid of every trace of blood. Luminol can generally detect it.

These tests only suggest the presence of blood. There can be false positives, so they must be used carefully in a court of law. But they may be a very useful first step in investigating a crime scene.

This scientist is performing a Kastle-Meyer test to determine if there is blood on the shoe.

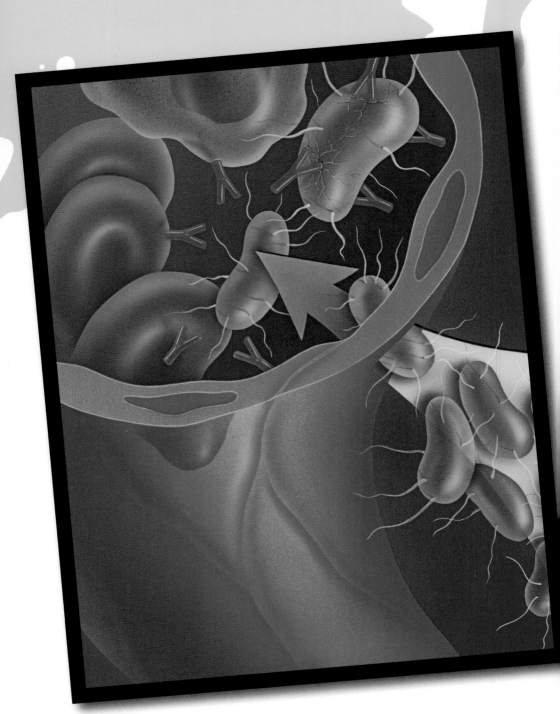

The illustration shows Y-shaped antibodies attaching to antigens on bacteria as they enter the bloodstream.

or horses was added to serum from the inoculated animal, the mixture remained clear. The rabbits had not formed antibodies against cow, pig, sheep, or horse antigens because they had only been injected with chicken blood. Uhlenhuth concluded that the blood of different animals had characteristic proteins not shared by the blood of other animals.

He showed that a rabbit injected with human blood—even dried blood—would produce a serum that reacted specifically with human blood. He immediately recognized just how important this test would be to forensic science. "Judges and experts have for a long time been most deeply concerned with the all-important problem of distinguishing human blood from other blood types," he wrote. "Until now, though, a sure answer to this question has been impossible [in the case of dried blood]. . . . Since in forensic practice one is almost exclusively concerned with such dried blood, one must be equipped

Scientists are able to determine whether blood at a crime scene is from a human or another animal.

with a practical, forensic method to determine also the origins of blood in this condition."[1]

Today, forensic scientists have a fast, easy-to-use version of Uhlenhuth's precipitin test to determine what species a blood sample came from. The test is so sensitive that it can detect tiny amounts of blood in a stain that is decades old.

Elementary, My Dear Watson

Arthur Conan Doyle introduced Sherlock Holmes to the world in 1887, with the publication of *A Study in Scarlet*. The detective had just discovered an infallible test for bloodstains:

> "I've found it! I've found it," he shouted to my companion, running towards us with a test-tube in his hand. "I have found a re-agent which is precipitated by haemoglobin, and by nothing else . . . . Criminal cases are continually hinging upon that one point. A man is suspected of a crime months perhaps after it has been committed. His linen or clothes are examined and brownish stains discovered upon them. Are they bloodstains, or mud stains, or rust stains, or fruit stains, or what are they? That is a question which has puzzled many an expert, and why? Because there was no reliable test. Now we have the Sherlock Holmes's test, and there will no longer be any difficulty."[2]

When *A Study in Scarlet* was first published, and probably for many years afterward, people thought that the Holmes Test was fictional. In 1987, Christine L. Huber showed that the Holmes Test was no mere storytelling device. Using chemicals that would have been available to Conan Doyle, Huber followed the procedure described in the story—and got the same results. "How [the test] was lost in the first place and

Fictional detective Sherlock Holmes and his partner,
Dr. Watson, check for evidence.

why Holmes never received acknowledgement for it remains a mystery," Huber wrote. "Perhaps it is enough, however, to know that in his centennial year Sherlock Holmes has been vindicated as the wisest and best chemist whom it has been our pleasure to know."[3]

Whose Blood?

Helen Priestly, a confident fair-haired girl, was well liked by everyone in the apartment building and neighborhood where she lived with her parents in Aberdeen, Scotland. Everyone, it seems, except Jeannie Donald. Her daughter had once been Helen's friend, but the girls had quarreled. The two families no longer spoke. Jeannie would scowl at Helen as she passed on the street and scold her when she played nearby. Helen, in turn, liked to taunt her neighbor with the nickname "Coconut," in reference to the woman's frizzy hair.

Early in the afternoon of April 20, 1934, Helen's mother sent her out to buy some bread at a nearby shop. When she failed to return, her

Aberdeen, Scotland

mother went out to look for her. Yes, said the shop staff, they had seen Helen. She had bought her loaf of bread around 1:30 P.M. Someone had seen her walking home around 1:45 P.M.

Within a few hours, the police and hundreds of local people turned out to look for Helen. Her body was found at five o'clock the next morning. It was stuffed in a large blue sack in the apartment building's common bathroom on the ground floor. She had been strangled. The police questioned everyone in the building. Jeannie Donald seemed to have an airtight alibi. She had been shopping the afternoon of Helen's disappearance, she said. But details of her story didn't pan out. The police searched the Donald apartment. They found what appeared to bloodstains, and the Donalds were soon behind bars. Mr. Donald's alibi held up, so he was released. Police attention rested solely upon Jeannie Donald.

They called in Sydney Smith, professor of forensic medicine at Edinburgh University, to help investigate. He turned his attention first to the blue sack in which Helen's body had been found. He found fibers of wool, cotton, silk, linen, and jute. There was cat, rabbit, and human hair. Some of the human hair matched Helen's, but some hairs were distinctly different. He examined all of them under a microscope, comparing them with samples taken from the Donald household and from other apartments in the building. He found twenty-five fibers in the Donald home that matched fibers from the blue sack. None of the other apartments had matching fibers.

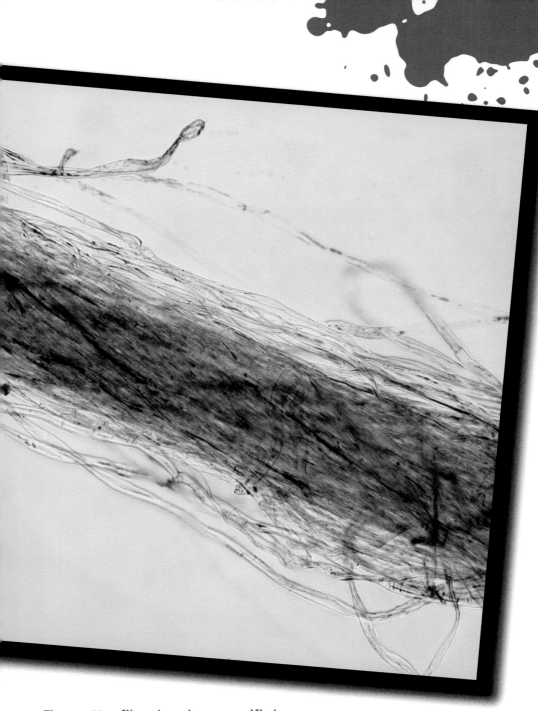

These cotton fibers have been magnified using a microscope. Do you think you could tell them from other types of fibers?

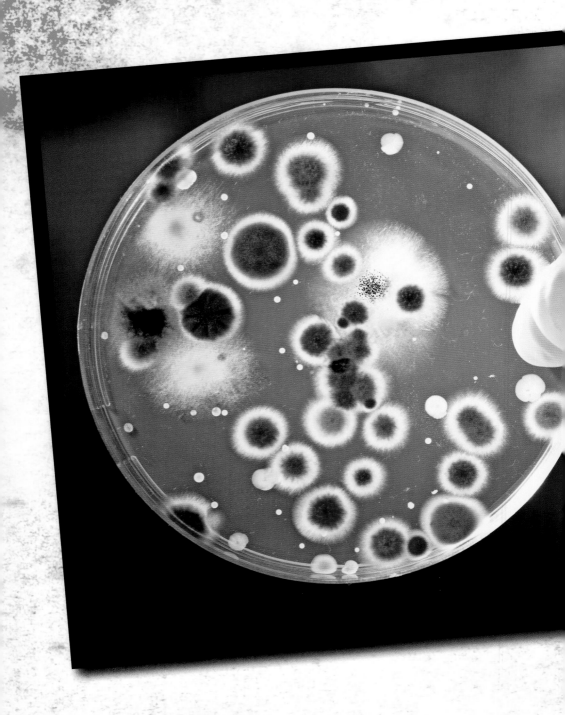

BACTERIAL FINGERPRINTING?

Sydney Smith was way ahead of his time in recognizing that individuals could be identified by the unique bacteria that live in their bodies. The typical human body is home to a huge number of microbes. In fact, there are ten times more microbial cells in your body than human cells! (You don't see the microbial cells when you look in the mirror because they're much smaller than human cells.) They live in our mouths and our intestines, and on our skin. Each of us carries with us a set of bacteria that is unique to us, in terms of the numbers and types of species and strains.

"Each one of us leaves a unique trail of bugs behind us as we travel through our daily lives," said Noah Fierer, an assistant professor at the University of Colorado at Boulder. Fierer and his colleagues took samples of bacteria deposited on the personal keyboards of different computer users. Using new gene-sequencing techniques, they created a DNA profile of all the bacteria deposited on those surfaces. They compared these bacterial DNA signatures to those from the hands and fingers of the computer users and of random people. The bacterial DNA taken from the keys of the computer owners matched that of the owners much more closely than that of samples taken from random keyboards and fingertips.

"While this project is still in its preliminary stages, we think the technique could eventually become a valuable new item in the toolbox of forensic scientists," Fierer said.[1]

Next, he turned his attention to some evidence that the police had missed. He found bloodstains on two washcloths, a cleaning brush, a package of soap, the floor, and a newspaper dated the day before the murder. His laboratory found the blood to be type O, the same as Helen Priestly's blood. Jeannie had type A blood. So far, everything seemed to point to Jeannie's guilt. But about half of the world's population has type O blood, so it would be impossible to prove that the blood was Helen's.

Then Smith had a brilliant idea. He knew that Helen's intestine had been split open during that attack. Knowing that we all carry billions of bacteria in our intestines, he guessed that some of the bacteria might have been released into Helen's blood. (There is normally no bacteria in blood.) Smith sent some of Helen's bloodstained clothing, along with the bloodstained articles from the Donald apartment, to a professor of bacteriology at Edinburgh University. The bacteriologist found considerable amounts of bacteria in Helen's bloodstained clothing and on the washcloths. But the clincher was that both Helen's blood and the washcloths contained a highly unusual strain of bacteria.

Smith proposed that Jeannie had had enough of Helen's taunting and had killed her in a fit of rage. He concluded that the washcloths had been used to mop up Helen's blood. The jury believed him, and Jeannie Donald was sentenced to life in prison.

Murder, Fingerprints, and Cigarette Butts

The Priestly-Donald case was the first one in which blood-typing played an important role in solving the case. In 1939, the young science of forensic serology seemed to take two steps forward and one step back in a famous case involving a murder, a glass, and cigarette butts.

On the night of May 21, 1939, a well-to-do businessman named Walter Dinivan was badly beaten in his apartment on the southern coast of England. He died later that night without regaining consciousness. Chief

Inspector Leonard Burt of Scotland Yard examined the crime scene carefully. All the evidence seemed to point to robbery: Dinivan's living room safe had been opened with his keys and emptied of its contents. A crumpled paper bag lay on the floor. There were two glasses resting on the table in the sitting room, suggesting Dinivan had been having a drink with someone. There also were a number of cigarette butts scattered about.

Inspector Burt examined the apartment for fingerprints, including on the glasses. He found fingerprints that matched Dinivan and various members of his family, of course. But there was a print on one of the glasses that didn't match any of the others. On the chance that the murderer was a **secretor**—a person whose blood antigens can also be found in his saliva—Inspector Burt had his lab test the cigarette butts. The lab results came back: The saliva residue on the cigarettes showed that whoever had smoked them had type AB blood. This is generally the rarest type of blood. It is found in just 3 percent of the Caucasian population.

In the course of interviewing Dinivan's family and acquaintances, the name of Joseph Williams came up. Williams had been a friend of the dead man. Unlike Dinivan, he was chronically broke, although he had come into a large sum of money around May 21. When questioned by the police, he admitted that he had been angry with Dinivan, who had refused to loan him some money. But he said that he won the money betting on a horse race. He refused to let the police get a sample of his fingerprints or to submit to a blood test.

Inspector Burt was a clever man, though. He ordered his officers to keep an eye on Williams and to let him know if his suspect entered a pub. A few days later, he got the call. The inspector rushed to the pub, where he "accidentally" ran into Williams. Burt offered him a drink and a cigarette, both of which Williams accepted. They chatted about horse racing for the next hour or so, and Burt kept Williams in a steady supply

In certain people called secretors, blood type can sometimes be determined from used cigarette butts!

of alcohol and cigarettes. After Williams staggered out of the bar, Burt carefully gathered the contents of the ashtray and had them sent to his lab to be tested for blood type.

Williams was a secretor. His blood type was AB.

Armed with this information, Burt searched Williams's apartment. He found a bundle of paper bags exactly like the one that had been found in Dinivan's apartment—which Burt suspected had been wrapped around the murder weapon. Williams insisted he was innocent, daring Burt to take his fingerprints. Burt did so, and found a match to the mystery print on the glass in Dinivan's apartment.

The money, the fingerprint, the rare blood type—the evidence against Williams seemed to be strong, even though there was no direct evidence to place him with Dinivan on the night of the murder. But forensic serology was still a fairly young science. At the trial, Williams's lawyer held up one of the cigarette butts.

In a blood-typing test, blood is mixed with antibodies to see how it reacts.

WHOSE BLOOD IS IT?

Around the same time Paul Uhlenhuth developed his precipitin method to distinguish animal blood from human blood, a fellow Viennese scientist named Karl Landsteiner made an important discovery. He found that human red blood cells carry certain sugar molecules, or antigens, that can vary from one person to another. Some people carry the A antigen on their red blood cells (they are type A), some carry the B antigen (type B), and some carry both (type AB). Some people carry neither the A nor the B antigen; they are type O.

To determine blood type, a scientist places a small sample of blood on each of two glass slides. She adds a drop of serum containing anti-A antibodies to one sample, and a drop of serum containing anti-B antibodies to the other. Anti-A antibodies cause type A blood cells to clump together, anti-B antibodies cause type B blood cells to clump, and both antibodies cause type AB blood cells to clump. Neither antibody will cause type O blood to clump.

In 1940, Landsteiner discovered that some people carry an antigen called the Rhesus (Rh) factor, so people can also be Rh-positive or Rh-negative. Scientists soon found that blood type was inherited. This made it a useful marker for determining family relationships. Nine years later, British scientists discovered that the nuclei of red blood cells from females—but generally not those from males—contain a structure called the Barr body. This would be another useful way of identifying blood samples. Since those early days, scientists have discovered other proteins and enzymes that vary among individuals. By testing for eight different blood factors, scientists can narrow down the chances that two unrelated people share the same blood profile to between 1 in 100 and 1 in 1,000.[2]

In the 1920s, a Japanese scientist named Saburo Sirai discovered that 80 percent of the population had these same blood group antigens in other bodily fluids. For these people, called secretors, investigators can determine blood type by testing body fluids, such as saliva, tears, or urine.

BLOOD TYPES OF PEOPLE IN THE U.S.[3]

O+	37%	O–	6%
A+	34%	A–	6%
B+	10%	B–	2%
AB+	4%	AB–	1%

How was it possible, he asked them, to determine a blood type from traces of saliva on a cigarette butt?

The jury found Williams not guilty.

That night, after an evening of drinking, Williams confessed to a reporter, "I've got to tell somebody. You see the jury was wrong . . . it was me."[4]

Clearly, serology could be a useful tool in forensic science—but only to a point. In some cases, blood-typing is more useful for excluding a particular suspect than for including another. Here's why: Say investigators test a bloody knife found at the scene of a stabbing murder. They find that on the knife there is a mixture of type AB blood, matching that of the victim, and type A blood from another individual. One suspect turns out to have type O blood, so clearly it was not his blood on the knife. Another suspect does have type A blood—but so do approximately 45 percent of all Caucasians! This is where a technique called DNA fingerprinting becomes critical. But that is a story for the next chapter.

4

The Xbox Murders

Erin Belanger and her boyfriend, Francisco "Flaco" Ayo-Roman, moved from Massachusetts to Deltona, Florida, in 2004. They found a house for rent with fruit trees in the backyard and a pretty pink bedroom that Belanger adored. Belanger, 22, and 30-year-old Ayo-Roman had found jobs at a nearby Burger King. They shared the house on Telford Lane with their friends Michelle Ann Nathan and Anthony Vega and a pet dachshund named George. Other friends, Robert "Tito" Gonzalez and Jonathan Gleason, sometimes stayed with them.

Belanger and Ayo-Roman had been living in Deltona only four months when Belanger discovered that someone was living illegally in her grandmother's winter home across town. The man, Troy Victorino, had left papers and credit card receipts bearing his name scattered around the place. Furious, Belanger gathered up his belongings—clothes,

Troy Victorino (right) was arrested for the so-called "Xbox murders."

drugs, CDs, and an Xbox game system—and took them to her house. She called the police.

Victorino, a man with a criminal record and a reputation for violence, rounded up six of his friends to retrieve his things from the house on Telford Lane. It would be too risky for him to go; he'd just gotten out of jail, and he knew that another brush with the law would put him right back behind bars. He waited in the shadows while three of his friends rang the doorbell. An argument broke out, and Belanger dialed 911. "I don't want problems," she told the operator. "Oh, my God. All I did was want to get people that were living in my nana's house out."[1]

After hearing that the police were on their way, Victorino and his friends fled—but not before slashing the tires of two vehicles in the driveway. "I want them dead," he said.[2]

Three days later, Victorino and three friends were seen shopping for aluminum bats at Walmart. A store clerk asked one of the men if they needed any help. No, the man said. "He had a nasty attitude," the clerk later said.[3] Another store employee recalled the men joking about using the bats to bash people's heads in.

Early in the morning of August 6, 2004, Christopher Carroll came by the house on Telford Lane. A friend from Burger King had sent him there to check up on Gonzalez, who hadn't shown up for work that morning. The door had been kicked in, and from the entrance of the doorway he could see three bodies. Music was blaring from the stereo. The house was in shambles. There was blood everywhere.

The police arrived to find the four men and two women who had been living at Telford Lane dead. George, the little dachshund, lay dead next to Belanger.

Investigators believed from the outset that the killer—or killers—had known the victims. Troy Victorino immediately came to mind.

Two days later police arrested Troy Victorino, Robert Cannon, Jerone Hunter, and Michael Salas for the six murders. Cannon, Hunter, and Salas all confessed to the crimes, but Victorino steadfastly maintained his innocence. Cannon had pleaded guilty in order to avoid the death penalty and was expected to testify against the other three men at the trial. However, he later refused to cooperate.

Nevertheless, all three men were found guilty of first-degree murder and other charges. The strongest testimony against Victorino at the trial came from Florida Department of Law Enforcement DNA expert Emily Booth Varan. She found blood on a pair of boots prosecutors believed Victorino had worn on the night of the killings. The stains contained "a DNA profile that matched Erin Belanger's standard," Varan said, adding that it would take 750,000 times the world population of 6 billion to find a similar match.[4] She also found a bloodstain on the heel of the left boot that matched the DNA profile of Vega, and a third that corresponded to that of Ayo-Roman. Most of the DNA from sweat and skin cells Varan recovered from inside the boot matched Victorino's profile. Bloody footprints matching the boots were found at the crime scene.

Varan also found blood from Nathan, Gonzalez, and Vega on Hunter's Nike sneakers.

The DNA evidence sealed the case; even Victorino's attorney admitted that it was damaging. Troy Victorino and Jerone Hunter were sentenced to death by lethal injection. Robert Cannon and Michael Salas are serving life sentences.

The massacre, which would become known nationwide as the "Xbox murders," was about more than simple revenge over a missing gaming system. A conversation Victorino had with a fellow inmate while awaiting trial points to a deeper motivation: hunger for respect. "He claims he is a Latin King," said the inmate. "He is this big gang leader and they basically disrespected him and he had to deal with that because they couldn't treat a King like that."[5]

DNA Profiling

Most people have twenty-three pairs of **chromosomes** packed into the **nucleus** of nearly every cell in their bodies (with the exception of red blood cells, which have no nucleus). One set of chromosomes comes from the mother's egg; the other comes from the father's sperm. Each chromosome contains a strand of tightly coiled DNA, which would resemble a twisted ladder with rungs if you were to stretch it out. The rungs of the ladder are made of bonded pairs of subunits called **nucleotides**. It would make a very long ladder indeed—roughly six feet in length, with 3 billion rungs, or **base pairs**.

There are four different types of nucleotide bases in DNA: **adenine** (A), **thymine** (T), **cytosine** (C), and **guanine** (G). Adenine always bonds with thymine, and cytosine always bonds with guanine. The nucleotides are arranged in sections called genes, which give instructions for making proteins. Because we inherit one gene from each parent, we have two copies, or **alleles**, of each gene. A short section of DNA from the gene coding for myoglobin (a form of hemoglobin found in muscle cells) looks like this:

GGAGGTGGGCAGGA
CCTCCACCCGTCCT[6]

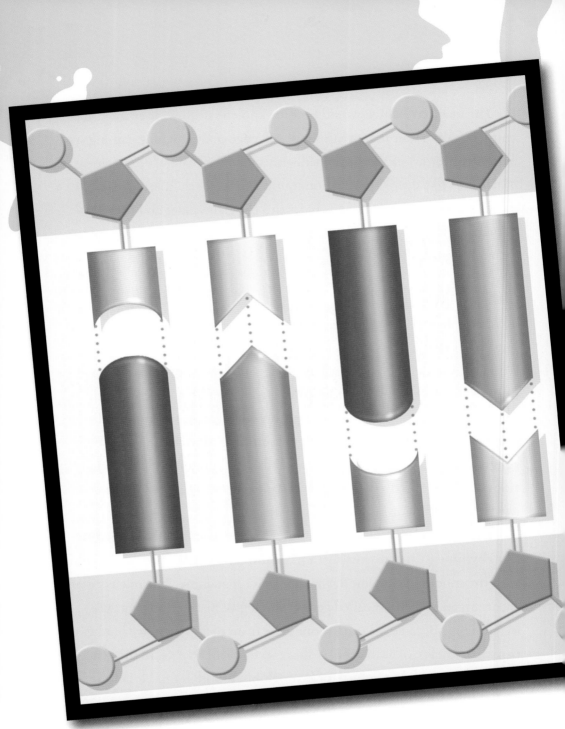

The diagram shows how nucleotides pair up in DNA.

The majority—99.9 percent—of human DNA is the same for all humans. Most of us share basic characteristics, after all: one head, two arms, two legs, 206 bones. But there are stretches of DNA, or loci, that do not appear to have any function—or, at any rate, do not code for any genes. These loci, called short tandem repeats (STRs), contain short segments of DNA that are repeated one after another in different numbers from one individual to another. Since these loci do not code for any genes, they can vary dramatically without affecting the health of an individual. STRs are used in DNA profiling. The technique was first used to solve a criminal case in 1987, when police in the United Kingdom collected blood samples from over 5,000 people in order to identify the man who had murdered two young women.

Let's say that crime scene investigators find skin cells under the fingernails of a woman who was murdered. They suspect that the skin came from the murderer, scratched off as the woman tried to fend off her attacker. The investigators may wear masks, disposable coveralls, and booties, and use gloves when collecting evidence. It is very important that the evidence does not become contaminated with DNA from the investigators or other people.

In the laboratory, scientists break up the skin cells and extract and purify the DNA. They copy the DNA and the thirteen STR regions that vary from person to person, using a polymerase chain reaction, or **PCR**, technology. Sometimes described as "molecular photocopying,"[7] PCR amplifies even minute amounts of DNA until there is enough material for analysis. This is especially useful if the sample is very small or old.

By determining the type of the sample's STR loci, forensic scientists create a DNA profile for the individual. Although there are over 2,000 STR loci that could be tested, only a few of them are routinely used for forensic DNA profiling. In the United States, the FBI (Federal Bureau

Laboratory technicians are trained to perform forensic blood tests.

of Investigation) uses thirteen markers. The likelihood that two people (with the exception of identical twins) will have the same DNA profile at all thirteen loci is one in 10 billion—or greater. Specific DNA profiles are stored in a computer database called the Combined DNA Index System (CODIS). Forensic laboratories all across the country have access to this database.

Armed with a DNA profile of the suspect, the forensic scientist searches for a match using CODIS. He strikes gold—the profile matches that of the woman's ex-boyfriend, who had been in the CODIS database after being convicted for an earlier crime.

DNA Databases

Katie Sepich, a graduate student at New Mexico State University, was murdered in 2003. There were no strong suspects, but investigators used skin and blood under her fingernails to create a DNA profile of her attacker. They entered the DNA profile into CODIS, but there were no matches.

Sepich's parents learned that most states allow law enforcement officials to take DNA only from people who have been convicted of a felony—not from those simply arrested for one. Just three months after Sepich's murder, a man named Gabriel Avilla was arrested, but not convicted, on a **felony** charge. When Avilla was convicted of another felony crime in 2006, his DNA profile was entered into CODIS. It matched that of Sepich's killer. Had the DNA sample been taken upon his first arrest, her parents said, their daughter's killer would have been found three years earlier. In 2006, the New Mexico state legislature passed "Katie's Law," which requires law enforcement officials to take DNA samples from most felony arrests. To date, seventeen other states have followed suit.

In a March 6, 2010, interview with John Walsh, the host of the TV show *America's Most Wanted*, President Barack Obama agreed that there should be a national database of DNA profiles of every person arrested, whether convicted or not. "We have eighteen states who are taking DNA upon arrest," Walsh said. "It's no different than fingerprinting or a booking photo. . . . "

"It's the right thing to do," President Obama said. "This is where the national registry becomes so important, because what you have in individual states—they may have a database, but if they're not sharing it with the state next door, you've got a guy from Illinois driving over into Indiana, and they're not talking to each other."[8]

Several countries, including England and Wales, do have national DNA databases of everyone who has been arrested for a crime. But many people believe that such databases violate an individual's right to privacy. They worry that it would unjustly target minorities. Bill Quigley of the Center for Constitutional Rights disputed Walsh's claim that taking DNA is no different from taking fingerprints. "It's like giving a blank check to the government—a blank check that they can cash anytime they feel like it," he said.[9]

Michael Seringhaus, a student at Yale Law School, wrote an editorial in the *New York Times* proposing that we keep every American's DNA profile on record. "A universal record would be a strong deterrent to first-time offenders," he wrote. "After all, any DNA sample left behind would be a smoking gun for the police—and would enable police to more quickly apprehend repeat criminals. It would also help prevent wrongful convictions. . . . Since every American would have a stake in keeping the data private and ensuring that only the limited content vital to law enforcement was recorded, there would be far less likelihood of government misuse than in the case of a more selective database."[10]

America's Most Wanted host, John Walsh

Y-CHROMOSOME ANALYSIS

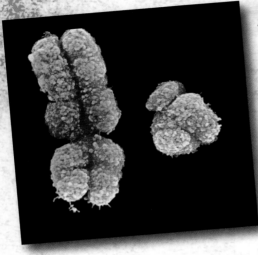

In most mammals, the sex of an offspring is determined by the X and Y chromosomes. Females have two X chromosomes—one inherited from each parent. Males have one X chromosome, inherited from the mother, and one Y chromosome, inherited from the father. Scientists have identified more than 200 STR loci on the Y chromosome; between nine and eleven of these markers may be used in forensic science. These markers are especially useful at crime scenes where there is a mixture of evidence from a male and female, or from several males. Because the Y chromosome is passed directly from a father to his sons, it can also be used to trace family relationships among males.

In 1998, Eugene Foster, a scientist at the University of Leicester in the U.K., used Y-chromosome analysis to help solve a centuries-old mystery. In 1802, President Thomas Jefferson was accused of fathering a child by his slave, Sally Hemings. The boy, called Thomas Woodson (he took the name of his later owner), was born in 1790. Jefferson denied it vigorously, but the rumors persisted. In 1808, Hemings gave birth to her last son, Eston, who was said to have borne a striking resemblance to Jefferson. As an adult, Eston entered white society in Madison, Wisconsin, going by the name Eston Hemings Jefferson. Eston Jefferson's descendents had always believed that Thomas Jefferson was the father of their ancestor, but most scholars believed that the father was one of the president's nephews. That would explain the resemblance to the president.

Foster realized the Y-chromosome analysis might help solve the mystery. President Jefferson and his wife, Martha, did not have any male children. But Jefferson did have an uncle on his father's side, Field Jefferson, who would have had shared Y-chromosome markers. Foster analyzed the Y chromosomes of five male-line descendants of Field Jefferson, six male-line descendents of Thomas Woodson and Eston Jefferson, and three male-line descendants of the presidents' nephews.

Foster found a rare marker on the Y chromosomes of Field Jefferson's descendants; so rare, in fact, that it has never been observed outside the Jefferson family. Thomas Woodson's descendants did not share the marker, but the descendant of Eston Jefferson did. The markers on the nephews' descendants were markedly different.

Foster concluded, "It is at least 100 times more likely if the president was the father of Eston Hemings Jefferson than if someone unrelated was the father."[11]

Descendants of Sally Hemings look at a family tree in Thomas Jefferson's historical home.

Questioning DNA Evidence

Even the most compelling DNA and blood evidence can be called into question if jurors can be convinced that investigators mishandled forensic evidence. This was the case in one of the most sensational and famous cases of the twentieth century, the murder trial of Orenthal James (O. J.) Simpson, a famous former football star and possibly one

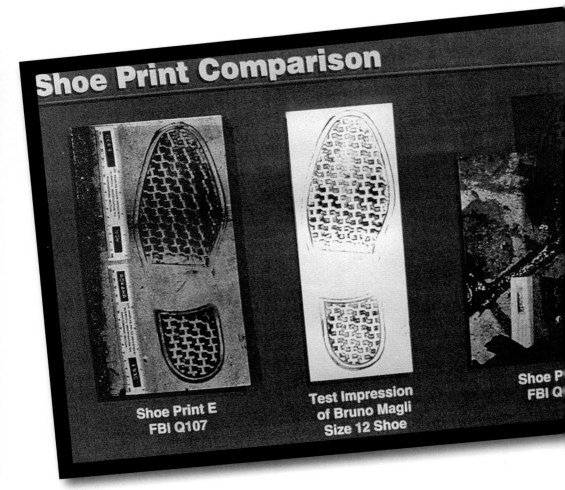

Shoe Print Comparison

Shoe Print E
FBI Q107

Test Impression
of Bruno Magli
Size 12 Shoe

Shoe P
FBI Q

This shoe print comparison was used during the trial of O. J. Simpson.

of the most well-known African Americans at the time. On June 12, 1994, the bodies of Simpson's ex-wife, Nicole Brown Simpson, and her friend Ronald Goldman were found just outside Nicole Simpson's Los Angeles apartment. Both had been brutally stabbed to death.

The Simpsons' seventeen-year relationship had been a rocky one, ending in divorce in 1993. They were not on good terms at the time the murders took place. O. J. Simpson was the prime suspect, and the case against him seemed airtight. A trail of bloody shoe prints at the murder scene that were made by the same size and make of shoes owned by Mr. Simpson contained DNA that matched his. A bloodstained left-handed glove found on Nicole Brown Simpson's property contained Mr. Simpson's DNA, as well as that of both victims. When the police questioned Mr. Simpson, they discovered a cut on his left hand. DNA from hair samples found on Mr. Goldman's body after the murder also matched Mr. Simpson's DNA. Blood in Mr. Simpson's Ford Bronco contained DNA from both Ms. Simpson and Mr. Goldman. A pair of bloodstained socks found in Mr. Simpson's bedroom contained Mrs. Simpson's DNA.

O. J. Simpson's trial lasted nine months and received widespread media coverage. Mr. Simpson's defense team included F. Lee Bailey, the lawyer who had successfully defended Sam Sheppard in his second murder trial. The defense lawyers targeted the honesty of the investigating police officers and the methods of the laboratories responsible for the DNA analysis. They claimed that some of the police officers were racist and might have planted evidence to incriminate their client. They also cast doubt upon the methods and competence of the laboratories that had carried out the DNA analysis. Despite the overwhelming evidence that Mr. Simpson had murdered his ex-wife and her friend, the jurors were not convinced that the blood samples had been handled appropriately. They found O. J. Simpson not guilty on both charges.

A detective points to a glove found near the blood-stained walkway at the scene of the murder of Nicole Brown Simpson.

Even though Mr. Simpson was found not guilty in a criminal court, Ron Goldman's family brought a civil case against the former football star. There is a lower threshold for proof of liability in a civil trial (in a civil court, defendants are found liable, rather than guilty). The lawyers did not have to prove that Simpson was guilty beyond a reasonable doubt—only that most of the evidence linked him to the murders. In this case, the jurors found Mr. Simpson liable of the murders and ordered him to pay $8.5 million in damages to the Goldman family.

The controversial O. J. Simpson trial highlights the importance of collecting and handling DNA evidence properly. Even the most compelling scientific evidence can be called into question if there is even a possibility that it might have been mishandled.

The Innocent Men

n April 1997, a man wearing a ski mask entered a convenience store in Bridge City, Louisiana, near New Orleans. He demanded money from the owner, Tommy Vanhoose. When the owner refused, the masked man shot and killed him. One witness was in her car at the time the masked man fled the store. She saw him briefly pull up his mask in the parking lot. He fired shots in her direction as he ran and dived through the open passenger window of a large primer-gray American-made car.

Two other witnesses, in a different car, said that the man had shed his mask, gloves, and shirt as he fled the scene. They confirmed that he was shooting his gun, and the driver of the car had seen the gunman's face in his rearview mirror.

Several hours later, eleven miles from the crime, two seventeen-year-old boys in a primer-gray 1981 Pontiac Grande Prix were pulled over by the police. Travis Hayes, the driver, and his friend, Ryan Matthews, were just driving around while listening to hip-hop music on the car stereo. The friends thought little of it at first; they had seen plenty of young black men pulled over by the police for seemingly no reason. But their car was similar to the description of the getaway car, and that made them prime suspects in Vanhoose's murder.

Hayes initially told police that he and Matthews had not been in the area where the murder had occurred. But after six hours of questioning, he changed his story. Hayes, who was mentally disabled, told investigators that he had driven with Matthews to the store and watched as his friend went inside. Fifteen minutes later, he said, he heard shots and saw Matthews run out. Matthews, on the other hand, maintained his innocence.

Two years later, Ryan Matthews went on trial for the murder of Tommy Vanhoose. His case seemed compelling. The defense presented evidence that the DNA from the inside of the ski mask did not match that of Matthews or Hayes. Witnesses said that the masked gunman had dived through the open car window, but the passenger window of the Grand Prix had been stuck closed for a long time. Other witnesses had described the perpetrator as short. Matthews was six feet tall.

THE INNOCENCE PROJECT

The Innocence Project, based in New York City, is an organization of attorneys and law students that use DNA technology to prove the innocence of people wrongfully convicted of serious crimes. As of September 16, 2010, 258 people who were previously convicted have been found innocent through DNA testing, including 17 people who had served time on death row.

Nevertheless, the jury was swayed by eyewitnesses who testified that Matthews was the man they had seen running out of the store. Hayes's confession seemed to confirm his guilt. Matthews was convicted of first-degree murder and sentenced to death. Hayes was convicted of second-degree murder and sentenced to life in prison without parole.

Matthews and Hayes, serving time in Louisiana's Angola prison farm, were desperate to prove their innocence. William Sothern and Clive Stafford Smith, attorneys with the Louisiana Crisis Assistance Center, thought that Matthews had not been given a fair trial. They appealed his case.

Sothern heard that a man in prison for an unrelated murder had been bragging to other prisoners about killing Tommy Vanhoose. The man, Rondell Love, had

TRUE CONFESSIONS?

It is hard to believe that people would confess to a crime they didn't commit. But according to the Innocence Project, defendants made incriminating statements, confessed, or pled guilty in about 25 percent of the cases where DNA evidence later proved their innocence. Why?

Confessions from children and teenagers, as well as those with mental disabilities, are often unreliable. Aggressive investigators easily influence them. Take the case of Michael Crowe, 14 years of age, who confessed to murdering his sister after an interrogation that lasted for hours. "Like I said, the only way I even know I did this is that she's dead and that the evidence says I did it. You could find that someone else did it, and I pray to God someone else did. I think it's too late for that. I think I did it."[1] DNA evidence later cleared Michael and the other two teens accused of the girl's death.

Harsh interrogation tactics, fear of violence and torture, and mental impairment due to alcohol or drug use are among the other reasons innocent people confess to crimes they didn't commit.

The Innocence Project says that the best way of preventing false confessions is to make electronic recordings of all interrogations. Recordings would improve the reliability of real confessions, it says, while protecting the rights of innocent suspects.

slashed the throat of a young woman named Chandra Conley just eight months after Tommy's murder. Sothern found that there was a DNA profile on file for Love. He compared Love's DNA profile with the DNA that had been found around the mouth of the ski mask. They were an exact match.

Ryan Matthews was granted a new trial. Based in part on the DNA evidence, the jury found him innocent of the charges. He was released from prison in 2004. He had become the fourteenth death row inmate in the United States to be proven innocent with DNA testing.

Even though Matthews had been declared innocent, Hayes remained in prison for two more years before attorneys at the Innocence Project managed to win his release. Together, the two men had served thirteen years in prison for a crime they did not commit.

After eight years in prison, Travis Hayes was released based on DNA evidence.

THE PROBLEM WITH EYEWITNESS TESTIMONY

It's a common scenario on crime television shows: The victim of a crime views a lineup of people matching the general description of the perpetrator. The victim studies each face carefully.

"Take your time," the police officer says.

The victim makes up her mind. "I think it's number four," she says.

"You're sure?" the officer asks.

She hesitates, and then nods. "Yes, I'm sure."

Just how reliable is eyewitness evidence? According to Elizabeth Loftus, a memory expert who has testified in more than 250 hearings and trials, memory is a tricky thing. Many of us have had the experience of hearing a family story so many times that we are sure we were there—only to learn that we were away at camp at the time it happened, or perhaps that the event took place before we were even born.

Loftus did an experiment in which she showed subjects six photos while they listened to a crime story. One out of the six photos showed the culprit; the other five were of innocent characters. Three days later, she showed the subjects a photo of one of the innocent characters, along with photos of three new people.

She asked them to pick the criminal from these four photos. Twenty-four percent of the subjects said that the criminal was not among the photos (the correct response). Sixteen percent picked one of the new characters. Sixty percent picked the most familiar face—the innocent character whose photo they'd seen both times.[2]

Mistaken eyewitness testimony can be triggered by subtle cues from police officers or detectives, a gap in memory, or a desire to make an identification at all costs. Loftus and other researchers have also found that if the perpetrator is not in the initial lineup, witnesses tend to pick somebody who resembles the criminal. They just assume that the real perpetrator is in the lineup, and it's their job to recognize him.

What does this mean for people like Ryan Matthews and Travis Hayes? Faulty eyewitness testimony is the single greatest cause of wrongful convictions nationwide, according to the Innocence Project. It plays a role in more than 75 percent of convictions overturned by DNA testing. Eyewitness testimony can be a valuable tool in the criminal justice system, but the Innocence Project has several recommendations:

- The person carrying out the photo or live lineup should not know who the real suspect is.

- "Fillers," or the nonsuspects in the lineup, should resemble the eyewitness's description of the criminal; one person shouldn't stand out too much from the others. Eyewitnesses should not view more than one lineup with the same suspect.

- The eyewitness should be told that the perpetrator might not be in the lineup.

- Immediately after the viewing the lineup, the eyewitness should give a statement about his or her confidence in the identification.

- Members in the lineup should be presented one at a time rather than all at once, if possible. Research has shown that this decreases the rate at which innocent people are picked out of a lineup.

6

New Tools Solve an Old Mystery

n the early morning of July 17, 1918, Tsar Nicholas II of Russia's Romanov family; his wife, Alexandra; their five children; three servants; and the family doctor were led to the cellar of a house in Ekaterinburg, Siberia, where they were held captive. The Romanov family had ruled Russia for 300 years, until the Bolsheviks (later known as Communists) took power in the 1917 Russian Revolution.

Once the family and staff were assembled in the cellar their captor, Yakov Yurovsky, called in a firing squad. He read from a piece of paper, "In view of the fact that your relatives are continuing their attack on Soviet Russia, the Ural Executive Committee has decided to execute you."[1] Yurovsky shot the tsar, who died immediately, and the firing squad shot and bayoneted the rest. The headline of the local newspaper read, "Execution of Nicholas, the Bloody Crowned Murderer—Shot Without

Bourgeois Formalities but in Accordance With Our New Democratic Principles."[2]

Six months later, a Russian investigator found several pieces of evidence from the supposed grave site, but no skeletons. The location of the remains of the Romanovs was a mystery until 1989, when two amateur Russian historians announced that they had located the grave, about twenty miles from Ekaterinburg. In 1991, the Russian government authorized an official forensic investigation of the grave. Investigators recovered 1,000 bone fragments that were assembled into five female and four male skeletons.

Russian forensic experts used computer software to superimpose the skulls with pictures of the Romanovs and their staff, compared the teeth with dental records, and measured the bones to determine the ages and sexes of the remains. They readily identified the bones of a middle-aged woman with expensive dental work as Alexandra. Likewise, they determined that the bones of a fairly short middle-aged man showing signs of wear and tear due to years of horseback riding (a favorite activity of the tsar) were those of Nicholas II.

The scientists identified the other four adult skeletons as the remains of the royal physician, the family cook, Nicholas's personal attendant (all male), and the maid.

The remaining three skeletons belonged to young adult or near-adult females. Forensic anthropologists determined that they probably belonged to the three oldest daughters, Olga, 22, Tatiana, 21, and Maria, 19. There was some dispute as to whether the skeleton identified as Maria's actually belonged to the youngest daughter, Anastasia, who was 17 at the time.

At any rate, two skeletons were missing: that of either Anastasia or Maria, and that of 13-year-old Alexei, the heir to the throne. The missing skeletons fueled mass speculation that Alexei and one of the two younger

The Romanov family was killed during an uprising in Russia. Only some of their remains were found, and for many years people believed that some of the children may have escaped.

daughters had somehow escaped execution and were living secret lives elsewhere.

To confirm the bone studies, government authorities asked a Russian biologist named Pavel Ivanov to carry out DNA testing on the bones. Knowing that they did not have the necessary technology to carry out the studies in Russia, Ivanov arranged to conduct DNA tests on the bones in collaboration with Peter Gill at the British Forensic Science Service. He flew from Moscow to London with pieces of the leg bones of each of the nine skeletons in his carry-on bag.

A television producer driving a funeral hearse met him at the airport. The producer felt that it was "inappropriate to carry the Russian Imperial family in the boot [trunk] of my Volvo."[3]

The scientists had their work cut out for them. The bones had deteriorated quite a bit, and there was not much DNA left to analyze. First, they determined the sex of each skeleton by analyzing a gene on the X chromosome that is six base pairs longer than the similar gene on the Y chromosome. They determined that there were four males and

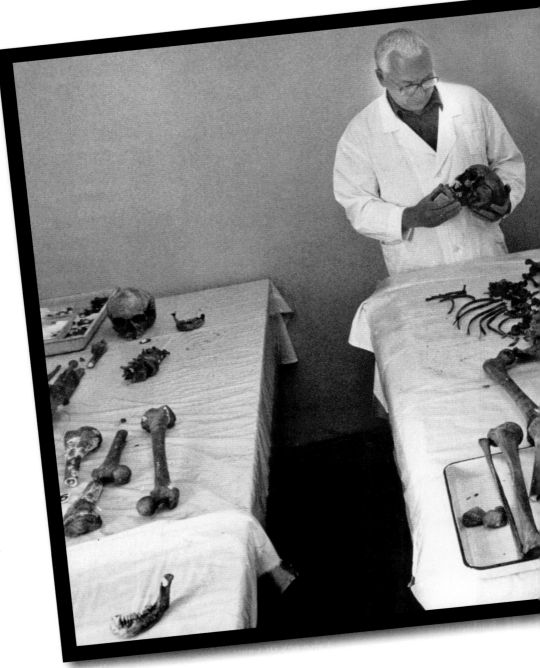

A forensic scientist examines the remains of the
Romanov family after they were found in the 1990s.

five females, confirming the forensic anthropologists' findings.

They used the recently developed PCR technique (described in Chapter 4) to amplify STR sequences. The STR patterns in the samples revealed a mother, a father, and their three daughters, as well as four unrelated adults. But they still had to prove that the bones were indeed those of the Romanov family.

For that they turned to mitochondrial DNA. Mitochondrial DNA, you will recall, is inherited only from the mother. The scientists had no problem creating a mitochondrial DNA profile for each of the nine skeletons. However, they needed to find living relatives of the Romanovs so they could compare the DNA profiles. Fortunately, Prince Philip, Duke of Edinburgh, was Alexandra's great-nephew (his mother, Princess Alice of Greece, was the daughter of Alexandra's older sister). Prince

Philip agreed to help, and sent Gill and Ivanov a test tube of his blood. The match was perfect: the mother, three daughters, and Prince Philip all shared the same mitochondrial DNA sequences.

Finding a reference sample for Nicholas proved more difficult. The tsar's nephew, Tikhon Kulikovsky, refused to cooperate. The scientists pored over Nicholas's family tree to find other relatives with the same maternal bloodline. They found two distant relatives, Xenia Sfiri and the Duke of Fife, who agreed to send blood samples.

The mitochondrial DNA of Xenia Sfiri and the Duke of Fife matched exactly. But when the scientists compared that DNA with the sample they thought belonged to the tsar, they found one mismatch out of 781 base pairs. Where Sfiri and the Duke of Fife had a thymine, Nicholas had a cytosine. Puzzled, the scientists ran the test again. This time, some of the genes matched those of Sfiri and the duke; others repeated the same mismatching cytosine. The scientists concluded that Nicholas had two forms of mitochondrial DNA, a condition known as **heteroplasmy** (at the time it was thought to be rare, but now scientists believe it to be fairly common). They published their results, saying that there was a 98.5 percent chance that these remains had belonged to Nicholas II.

But doubts about the identity of the bones presumed to be those of Nicholas II remained. And so, in 1994, the scientists were given permission to analyze the DNA from the body of Nicholas's brother, Georgij, who had died in 1899 from tuberculosis. They analyzed the brother's DNA and found that he had the exact same rare forms of two mitochondrial DNA. The mystery of five members of the Romanov family finally was laid to rest. But what of the two children who were unaccounted for? Was it possible that they had survived? It seemed unlikely that Alexei could have survived—he had a medical condition called hemophilia that prevented his blood from clotting. Even if he hadn't died from the gunshot wounds, he would surely have bled to death.

In the years following the execution, several women claimed to be Anastasia, the missing Romanov daughter. One "Anastasia" stood out from the rest. In 1920, a year and a half after the Romanov murders, a young woman jumped from a bridge into a Berlin canal. A policeman rescued her and took her to the hospital. She had no identification and refused to give her name. She was later transferred to a mental hospital in Germany. While she was there, she said that she was Grand Duchess Anastasia. She said that when the bodies of her family were carried out of the cellar, one of the soldiers had noticed that she was injured but alive. The soldier and his brother and mother helped smuggle her out of the country. She had come to Berlin, she said, to seek help from Empress Alexandra's sister Princess Irene of Prussia. She had thrown herself into the canal after becoming convinced that her aunt would not recognize her.

In fact, upon viewing the young woman, Princess Irene did not recognize her. "I saw immediately that she could not be one of my nieces," Irene wrote. "Even though I had not seen them for nine years, the fundamental facial characteristics could not have altered to that degree, in particular the position of the eyes, the ears, and so forth."[4]

In 1927, a German woman said that Anna, as the prospective Anastasia was now called, was actually Franziska Schanzkowska. She said that Franziska, a Polish factory worker whose family were peasants, had been a lodger in her mother's home until her abrupt disappearance in 1920. Even so, Anna had many supporters who believed her story, including the son of the Romanov family doctor. Anna eventually moved to Charlottesville, Virginia, where she went by the name Anna Anderson. She held fast to her story until her death in 1984.

After the 1991 finding that the bones of Alexei and one of the sisters were missing from the grave site, there was renewed interest in Anna's identity. Although her body had been cremated, a hospital in Charlottesville still had some tissue samples that had been removed following

MITOCHONDRIAL DNA ANALYSIS

Although most DNA resides within the nucleus of the cell, there is another important place to find DNA in the cell—the **mitochondria**. Mitochondria are tiny structures that transform oxygen and nutrients into energy to power the cell. The number of mitochondria in each cell varies according to its energy needs; liver cells, for example, contain between one thousand and two thousand of these little powerhouses.

Each mitochondrion carries two to ten copies of DNA to help carry out its functions. Regular DNA comes from both parents, but mitochondrial DNA (mtDNA) comes just from the mother. Although both the mother's egg cells and the father's sperm cells carry mtDNA, the father's mtDNA gets left outside of the egg cell after fertilization. This means that all of the mtDNA in the cells of an individual's body are copies of his or her mother's mtDNA. Mitochondrial DNA contains just 16,569 base pairs (compared with the 3 billion base pairs in nuclear DNA), but it can be very useful in some forensic cases.

Because mtDNA analysis is not as definitive as STR analysis, it is often used when samples cannot be analyzed using conventional methods. Old hair, bone, and tooth cells, for example, lack high-quality DNA in the nucleus. If the biological evidence is highly degraded, there may very well be enough intact mtDNA left to analyze. And finally, because mtDNA is inherited through the mother's line, scientists can help solve a cold case by analyzing and comparing the mtDNA profile of unidentified remains with any maternal relative. The FBI started using mtDNA analysis to solve cold cases in 1996.

an operation on her intestine. After a yearlong battle over who had the rights to test the tissue sample, it went to Peter Gill. Comparing the DNA in the tissue sample to Prince Philip's DNA, he declared that Anna Anderson was not related to the Romanov family. In 1994, Gill confirmed that Anna Anderson was not related to the Romanov family when he compared the DNA from the tissue sample to that of Karl Maucher, a relative of Franziska Schanzkowska. It was, he said, "a 100 percent match, an absolute identity."[5]

The final piece of evidence was uncovered in 2007, when a group of amateur archaeologists discovered a second grave just 70 meters from the original Romanov burial site. The grave held charred bone fragments and teeth of an adolescent boy and of a girl that had been somewhat older. The Russian government asked an international team of scientists to carry out DNA testing on the bones. They reconstructed the entire mitochondrial gene sequences of the bones, conducted STR analysis on the nuclear DNA, and analyzed Y-chromosome markers of the male bones. The results were clear: These were the bones of the missing children, Alexei and one of his sisters.

After ninety years, cutting-edge DNA forensics has finally solved one of the most enduring mysteries of the twentieth century.

Wildlife Forensics

Samuel K. Wasser, a conservation biologist at the University of Washington, discovered two elephant skulls lying side by side in a game reserve in Tanzania, a country in central East Africa. One skull had belonged to a baby elephant—its small teeth had not yet been used enough to show signs of wear. The other, larger skull had belonged to a female. One detail caught Wasser's eye. The dental pattern of the two skulls was almost identical; the only difference was the size of the teeth. Clearly, the adult and baby elephants had been related.

He understood immediately what had happened. Knowing that family ties are very strong among elephants, poachers had killed the baby elephant in order to draw the grieving mother elephant close enough to kill her. They cut off her enormous tusks (actually just very long teeth), leaving the two bodies to rot. Her ivory tusks would later

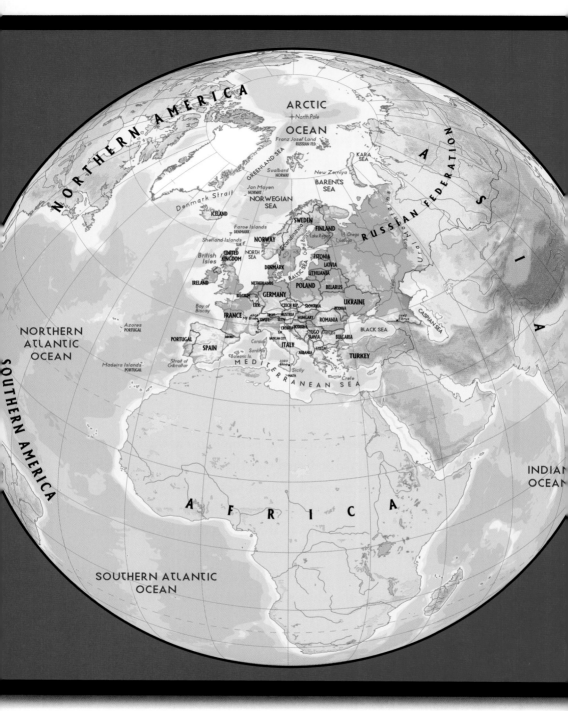

Populations of elephants in Africa are declining due to illegal poaching.

be sold and carved into ornamental objects.

This and other equally horrific scenarios have been played out thousands of times in past decades across much of Africa. In 1979, there were an estimated 1.3 million African elephants; today, only 470,000 remain. The decline is due in part to habitat loss as human populations in Africa rise. But rampant poaching is the main reason for the dwindling numbers of African elephants.

In 1989, the Convention on International Trade in Endangered Species (CITES, a United Nations organization) banned international trade in ivory. Demand for ivory dried up, and for a time it seemed as though elephants might be safe from poachers.

That all changed during the 1990s. Three African countries—Botswana,

IVORY IN THE DONUT SHOP

When U.S. Fish and Wildlife Service special agents searched Moun Chau's donut shop in Claremont, California, in 2007, they found more than just glazed donuts and apple fritters. Following an undercover operation, they seized dozens of ivory items worth thousands of dollars. Chau had purchased the ivory, advertised for sale on eBay, from a Thai businessman named Samart Chokchoyma. The businessman shipped the goods to Chau in packages marked as toys. Scientists at the U.S. Fish and Wildlife Service Forensics Laboratory in Ashland, Oregon, used DNA testing to confirm that the ivory had come from African elephants. In January 2010, U.S. authorities arrested Chau. Chokchoyma was arrested by Thai police. Both men were charged with several crimes, including violating the U.S. Endangered Species Act. Even so, officials don't believe that Chokchoyma was the ringleader of the ivory smuggling gang, which probably includes members from several countries. But it's a start.

It is illegal to traffic in ivory elephant tusks.

Namibia, and Zimbabwe—persuaded CITES to place elephants on a less endangered status, and to allow them to sell their stockpiled ivory abroad. Around the same time, people in some Asian countries—especially Thailand, China, and Japan—were becoming more prosperous. Beautiful objects carved from ivory were a status symbol—a sign that their owners had finally achieved wealth. Demand for ivory soared as money to enforce the laws diminished. Powerful and well-armed gangs of poachers and ivory traders began killing elephants by the thousands. They bribed corrupt customs officials and hid ivory in shipment containers that were shuttled between as many as half a dozen countries between Africa and Asia in order to avoid detection.

By 2006, poaching had become worse than ever before. In that year, law enforcement agents seized between 25,000 and 29,000 kilograms of illegal ivory. Based on these numbers, Wasser estimated that 38,000 elephants—more than 8 percent of the entire African elephant population—were being killed each year. The price of ivory has increased from $100 per kilogram in the 1990s to $1,800 per kilogram today.

Ivory elephant tusks can be worth lots of money.

"If the illegal ivory trade is not brought under control soon, most of Africa will lose the majority of its free-ranging elephants, and Africa will never be the same," Wasser wrote in a *Scientific American* article. "That is too great a price to pay for a commodity whose principal use is vanity."[1]

Until recently it was nearly impossible to track down poachers. If law enforcement agents seized an illegal shipment of ivory, they had no way of telling where it had come from. Dealers could claim that their ivory came from domesticated Asian elephants, which is legal. (Poachers have not targeted Asian elephants as much because only some male Asian elephants grow tusks, and females never do.) But now law enforcement officials have a new tool to help them track down the origin of the ivory: DNA profiling.

Over a decade, with the help of many scientists and game wardens, Wasser collected hundreds of elephant dung samples from all across sub-Saharan Africa. Each sample, containing DNA from millions of cells shed from the elephant's intestine, was shipped back to Wasser's lab at

THE CAVIAR CROOKS

Sturgeon—some twenty-six related fish species living in the rivers, lakes, and coastlines of the Northern Hemisphere—are sometimes called "living dinosaurs." It is not because of their large size, although they can reach 15 feet in length, and can weigh up to 2,500 pounds. Nor is it because of the spikes that run down their backs like those of a Stegosaurus. Sturgeon, and the related paddlefish, have been around since the age of the big dinosaurs 200 million years ago. These giants continued to thrive long after the dinosaurs died out. But today, many species of sturgeon and paddlefish are in trouble. It's all because humans have developed a taste for their eggs, or caviar. A breeding-age female can carry 5 million eggs—up to 20 percent of her body weight.

Unfortunately for the fish, harvesting sturgeon eggs isn't as easy as, say, gathering chicken eggs. Generally, people catch the slow-moving fish, club it over the head, and cut out its egg sacs. Later, they slaughter it for its meat. The world's best caviar comes from sturgeon living in the Caspian Sea (actually a salty lake), located in western Asia. In recent years, pollution and overfishing have greatly depleted the stock of breeding-age female sturgeon in the Caspian Sea. The harvest and sale of caviar from the three major species of sturgeon in the Caspian Sea is tightly regulated. Caviar from the beluga species, the most highly prized type of caviar, can no longer be legally exported to the United States. Not surprisingly, the price of caviar has skyrocketed—along with the activity of caviar criminals.

In 1999, special agents for the U.S. Fish and Wildlife Service's law enforcement division noticed that Sutton Place Gourmet, a specialty food store in Rockville, Maryland, was selling "Russian" Sevruga caviar for an unusually low price. This bargain smelled downright fishy to the agents. They bought some tins of the caviar and sent them to the Fish and Wildlife Service's National Forensics Laboratory in Oregon for DNA testing. The results showed that the eggs actually came from the American paddlefish, a protected species found in the Tennessee and Mississippi Rivers. Paddlefish caviar is not as expensive, but it can be passed off as Sevruga caviar to an uninformed consumer. The agents determined that Sutton Place Gourmet and other retailers were being duped by their New York–based supplier, Connoisseur Brands, and set up a sting operation to catch Alfred Yazbak, the president of the company.

A Fish and Wildlife agent posing as a fisherman offered to sell Yazbak paddlefish roe (eggs). (The agent used roe that had been seized in another illegal harvesting operation.) He warned Yazbak that it was illegal, but Yazbak bought it anyway. In a tape-recorded conversation, Yazbak told the phony fisherman that he wanted to purchase Paddlefish roe for years to come, since "I think that's the score to be made over the next five or six years."[2] In a related undercover operation, Yazbak was also found to have purchased black-market caviar smuggled out of Russia in suitcases.

The sting operations yielded enough evidence to convict Yazbak of conspiring to smuggle protected sturgeon caviar and of selling counterfeit caviar to retail food companies with false labels. He was sentenced to two years in prison, and he and his company were fined $160,000.

the University of Washington. He analyzed sixteen separate short tandem repeats (STRs) of DNA to create a reference profile for the elephant genome. Armed with the DNA profiles of dung samples from known geographic areas, and knowing that the genetic makeup of elephants living close to each other is more similar than elephants living far apart, Wasser was able to create a genetic map of the animals.

In 2002, customs agents opened a set of shipping crates supposedly carrying soapstone and found 6.5 tons of ivory—representing as many as 6,000 dead elephants. The crates had come from Zambia, although government officials there said that only 135 elephants had been killed inside their borders in 10 years. It was time for Wasser and his colleagues to put elephant DNA profiling to the test. Using techniques borrowed from dental forensics, they chilled peanut-sized pieces of ivory to −250 degrees Celsius (the low temperature preserves the DNA) and then smashed them to a powder. They extracted DNA from the powder, determined the STR alleles, and compared them to their reference database. They found that the tusks had come from Zambia. Although no arrests were made, the findings so embarrassed the chief of the Zambian wildlife department that he quit his job.

In 2006, authorities seized nearly eleven metric tons of elephant ivory from Taiwan, Hong Kong, and Japan. Officials from Taiwan and Hong Kong sent samples of the seized ivory to Wasser's lab in Washington. These tusks had come from elephants in Tanzania and northern Mozambique. At a CITES meeting in March 2010, both Zambia and Tanzania asked to be allowed to sell ivory that had been stockpiled, arguing that they had elephant poaching and the illegal ivory trade well under control. The delegates at the meeting turned both countries down, based in part on the DNA evidence. Conservation experts say that even legal trade in elephant tusks just adds to the desire for more ivory, encouraging even more poaching and illegal trade.

Careers

I f you are curious, detail-oriented, good at solving puzzles, and a fan of science, you may find a career in forensic science very rewarding. You will need a bachelor's degree in a science field—chemistry, biology, or physics. Forensic scientists who testify in court need good speaking skills, so joining a debate team or taking a course in public speaking are both good ideas.

There are several career specialties available to people interested in DNA and blood forensics. Criminalists analyze, identify, and interpret physical evidence. To become a certified criminalist, you must have a bachelor's degree in the physical or natural sciences.

If you are interested in DNA testing, you should take courses in genetics, molecular biology, statistics, and biochemistry. You also need two years of experience working in a forensics laboratory, and you must pass a certification examination. Criminalists work in forensic laboratories in police departments, sheriff's offices, district attorney's offices, regional and state agencies, medical examiners and coroner's offices, private companies, or colleges and universities. They may also work for

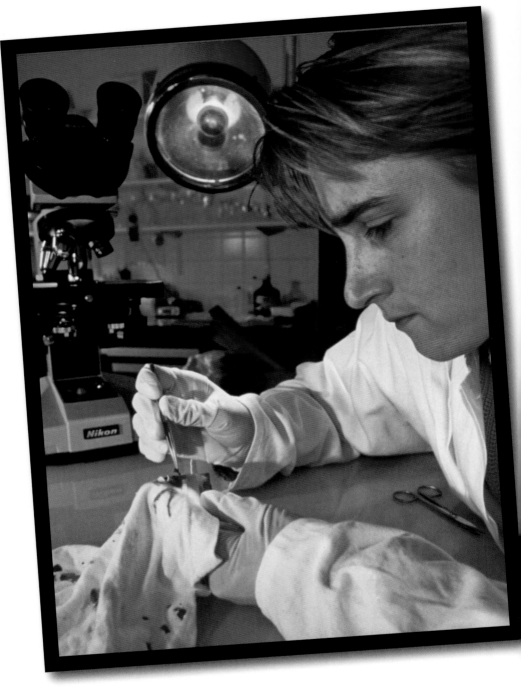

Forensic scientists gather lots of evidence and conduct many tests. This scientist is using a piece of fabric to extract blood for DNA evidence.

federal agencies, such as the Federal Bureau of Investigation, the Central Intelligence Agency, the military, or the U.S. Fish and Wildlife Service.

Crime scene investigators must have a bachelor's degree, either in a physical or a natural science, or in criminal justice. They assess, document, and gather evidence at crime scenes; view autopsies; meet with law enforcement officials; prepare detailed crime scene reports; and testify in court. Experts in bloodstain pattern analysis have a good working knowledge of math, physics, biology, and chemistry. They may work for many of the same agencies that employ criminalists, but the difference is that they do more fieldwork.

Income and job opportunities vary greatly depending on your degree, your specialty, and where you work. The mean annual wage for forensic scientists in 2009 was $55,070.[1] The U.S. Bureau of Labor Statistics expects to see employment opportunities for forensic science technicians increase by 20 percent over the next decade.

CHAPTER NOTES

Chapter 1. Blood Evidence

1. Fred McGunagle, "Sam Sheppard," *True Crime Library: Criminal Minds and Methods,* n.d., <http://www.trutv.com/library/crime/notorious_murders/famous/sheppard/index_1.html>(April 16, 2010).

2. Ibid.

3. Cynthia L. Cooper and Sam Reese Sheppard, *Mockery of Justice: The True Story of the Sheppard Murder Case* (Boston: Northeastern University Press, 1995), p. 112.

Chapter 2. The Case of the Bloody Carpenter

1. Paul Uhlenhuth, "Concerning my new forensic method to identify human blood," *Sourcebook in Forensic Serology, Immunology, and Biochemistry. Unit IX: Translations of Selected Contributions to the Original Literature of Medicolegal Examinations of Blood and Body Fluids* (National Institute of Justice, Research Foundation of the City University of New York, 1983), p. 177.

2. Sir Arthur Conan Doyle, "A Study in Scarlet," *Sherlock Holmes: The Complete Novels and Stories,* Volume 1 (Bantam Dell/Random House, 2003), pp. 7–8.

3. Christine L. Huber, "The Sherlock Holmes Blood Test: The Solution to a Century-old Mystery," *Sherlock Holmes by Gas-Lamp: Highlights From the First Four Decades of the Baker Street Journal* (New York: Fordham University Press, 1989), pp. 95–101.

Chapter 3. Whose Blood?

1. University of Colorado at Boulder, "New hand bacteria study holds promise for forensics identification." *ScienceDaily,* March 16, 2010, <http://www.sciencedaily.com/releases/2010/03/100315161718.htm> (April 16, 2010).

2. Alan Gunn, *Essential Forensic Biology*, 2nd Edition (West Sussex, U.K.: Wiley-Blackwell, 2009), p. 48.

3. United Blood Services. © 2008-2010. Human Blood Types. <http://www.unitedbloodservices.org/learnMore.aspx> (January 12, 2011).

4. Colin Evans, *The Casebook of Forensic Detection: How Science Solved 100 of the World's Most Baffling Crimes* (New York: John Wiley & Sons, 1996), p. 210.

Chapter 4. The Xbox Murders

1. Andrew Lyons, "Terror on Telford Lane. Part IV: An already tense situation escalates," *news-journalonline.com*, April 9, 2006, <http://www.news-journalonline.com/special/deltonadeaths/frtHEAD02040906.htm> (March 25, 2010).

2. Ibid.

3. Ibid.

4. Patricio G. Balona, "DNA testimony strongest yet in Deltona murder trial," *news-journalonline.com*, July 19, 2006, <http://www.news-journalonline.com/special/deltonadeaths/frt-HEAD02071906.htm> (March 31, 2010).

5. Patricio G. Balona, "Inmate: 'Disrespect' spurred Victorino to kill," *news-journalonline.com*, November 8, 2005, <http://www.news-journalonline.com/special/deltonadeaths/03AreaWEST01110805.htm> (March 31, 2010).

6. Alec J. Jefferys, "Genetic Fingerprinting," *Nature Medicine*, Vol. 11, No. 10, October 2005, pp. 1035–1039.

7. Henry C. Lee, Ph.D., and Frank Tirnady, *Blood Evidence: How DNA is Revolutionizing the Way We Solve Crimes* (Cambridge, Mass.: Perseus Publishing, 2003), p. 6.

8. White House Blog, "President Obama on 'America's Most Wanted,'" March 6, 2010, <http://www.whitehouse.gov/blog/2010/03/05/president-obama-americas-most-wanted> (May 30, 2010).

9. Josh Gerstein, "President Obama backs DNA test in arrests," Politico, n.d., <http://www.whitehouse.gov/blog/2010/03/05/president-obama-americas-most-wanted> (May 30, 2010).

10. Michael Seringhaus, "To Stop Crime, Share Your Genes," *New York Times*, March 15, 2010, p. A21.

11. Eugene A. Foster, et. al., "Jefferson fathered slave's last child," *Nature*, Vol. 396, November 5, 1998, pp. 27–28.

Chapter 5. The Innocent Men

1. Edwin Dobb, "False Confessions: Scaring Suspects to Death," *Amnesty Magazine*, n.d., <http://www.amnestyusa.org/amnestynow/false_confessions.html> (May 28, 2010).

2. William Saletan, "Leading the Witness: Contaminated Memories and Criminal Justice," *Slate.com*, May 26, 2010, <http://www.slate.com/id/2251882/pagenum/2> (May 30, 2010).

Chapter 6. New Tools Solve an Old Mystery

1. Robert K. Massie, *The Romanovs: The Final Chapter* (New York: Random House, 1995), p. 5.

2. Ibid., pp. 23–24.

3. Ibid., p. 82.

4. Ibid., p. 167.

5. Frances Welch, *A Romanov Fantasy: Life at the Court of Anna Anderson* (New York: W. W. Norton, 2007), p. 321.

Chapter 7. Wildlife Forensics

1. Samuel K. Wasser, Bill Clark, and Cathy Laurie, "The Ivory Trail," *Scientific American*, July 2009, p. 76.

2. U.S. Department of Justice, "Caviar Company and President Convicted in Smuggling Conspiracy," *FindArticles.com*, May 24, 2010, <http://findarticles.com/p/articles/mi_pjus/is_200201/ai_1061756705/> (May 31, 2010).

Chapter 8. Careers

1. Bureau of Labor Statistics, *Occupational Employment and Wages, May 2009, Forensic Science Technicians,* May 2009, <http://www.bls.gov/oes/current/oes194092.htm> (May 31, 2010).

GLOSSARY

adenine—One of the four bases in a DNA molecule; adenine (A) always pairs with thymine (T).

allele—One of two or more different forms of a gene at a specific position on the chromosome.

angle of impact—The angle between the direction of a blood drop and the plane of the surface it strikes.

antibody—A protein produced in response to and that neutralizes a specific antigen.

antigen—A molecule that induces an immune response in the body.

base pair—Two complementary nucleotide bases held together by a hydrogen bond in the DNA molecule; e.g., adenine-thymine, guanine-cytosine.

blood—The red liquid that circulates in arteries and veins and that carries oxygen to and carbon dioxide from the tissues of the body.

bloodstain pattern analysis—The science of studying the patterns left by blood on various surfaces in order to determine the events that led to their creation.

chromosomes—The structures in the nucleus of most cells that carry the genes that are transmitted from one generation to the next.

CODIS—Combined DNA Index System, the national DNA database that contains genetic profiles from convicted felons as well as profiles obtained from crime scene evidence.

cytosine—One of the four bases in a DNA molecule; cytosine (C) always pairs with guanine (G).

defense attorney—During a lawsuit or criminal prosecution, the attorney, or lawyer, who represents the defendant. Sometimes just called "the defense."

deoxyribonucleic acid (DNA)—The molecule that carries the genetic blueprint of an organism. It is made of two chains of the nucleotides adenine, cytosine, guanine, and thymine, as well as phosphate and sugar molecules.

enzyme—A molecule that helps bring about a specific chemical reaction.

felony—A serious crime that results in punishment by death or a sentence of greater than one year in a state or federal prison.

first-degree murder—The killing of a person with a deliberate plan while doing another crime.

gene—A sequence of DNA nucleotides on a chromosome that contains the information to make a protein.

genome—The total genetic makeup of an organism.

guanine—One of the four bases in a DNA molecule; guanine (G) always pairs with cytosine (C).

hemoglobin—A red protein, bound to an iron atom, responsible for transporting oxygen in blood.

heteroplasmy—The presence of more than one type of mitochondrial DNA within the same individual.

inquest—A legal inquiry in the presence of a judge or coroner to determine certain facts relating to an incident such as a death.

locus (plural loci)—The specific location of a gene or coding sequence on a chromosome.

mitochondrion (plural mitochondria)—A cellular structure, found in large numbers in cells, responsible for producing energy.

mitochondrial DNA—The genome found within mitochondria; it is passed on intact from a mother to her children.

nucleotide—One of the building blocks of DNA.

nucleus—A structure containing DNA that is found in most cells.

PCR (polymerase chain reaction)—A technique used to make many copies of DNA for analysis.

prosecuting attorney—The attorney, or lawyer, appointed by the government of a state to prosecute someone for a criminal case. Sometimes just called "the prosecution."

protein—A class of molecules made up of amino acids that provide the building blocks for much of the structure and function of the body.

second-degree murder—A death resulting from an assault in which the motive was not to kill the victim.

secretor—An individual who carries his or her blood group antigens in body fluids, including saliva and sweat.

serology—The study of blood and other bodily fluids.

serum—The clear yellowish liquid obtained after separating whole blood into its solid and liquid components after it has been allowed to clot.

spatter—The pattern made on a surface by drops of blood.

STR (short tandem repeat)—Short repeat units, two to seven bases long, that are connected to each other. STRs are usually located in between genes and often vary widely from one individual to another.

thymine—One of the four bases in a DNA molecule; thymine (T) always pair with adenine (A).

verdict—The official proclamation of decision by a jury.

FURTHER READING

BOOKS

Conklin, Barbara Gardner. *Encyclopedia of Forensic Science: A Compendium of Detective Fact and Fiction.* Westport, Conn.: Oryx Press, 2002.

Hauck, Max M. *Science Versus Crime.* New York: Facts on File, 2008.

Neme, Laurel A., Ph.D. *Animal Investigators: How the World's First Wildlife Forensics Lab is Solving Crimes and Saving Endangered Species.* New York: Scribner, 2009.

Stefoff, Rebecca. *Crime Lab.* New York: Benchmark Books, 2010.

Wagner, E. J. *The Science of Sherlock Holmes: From Baskerville Hall to the Valley of Fear, the Real Forensics Behind the Great Detective's Greatest Cases.* Hoboken, N. J.: John Wiley & Sons, 2006.

INTERNET ADDRESSES

American Academy of Forensic Sciences
<http://www.aafs.org/>

The DNA Initiative: Advancing Criminal Justice Through DNA Technology
<http://www.dna.gov/>

U.S. Fish & Wildlife Service Forensics Laboratory
<http://www.lab.fws.gov/>

INDEX